Meaningless

STAR

Meaningless

Fuck

Verb: ruin or damage (something)
- Treat (someone badly) or unfairly

Vulgar Slang!

You

> Pronoun: sucker reading this sentence

Meaningless

Read the first two pages again.

By the way, look down, always remember to tie your shoes! Life lessons.

To anyone as deranged as me.

August 27, 2022, 2:54 PM

I want a love that transcends time.
Where I love this person in every universe,
Every setting,
Every frigid field, I'll run.
However,
I haven't found that person yet.
I may never.

Sptember 13, 2022, 11:10 AM

Funny how my brain looks on cement.

September 14, 2022, 8:07 AM

I don't know what love is,
It comes in all forms.
I don't know what romantic love is.
It goes from no touching,
To PDA,
Spending every second with each other,
Or only seeing each other in bed.
Not talking to each other,
Or talking too much.
Pulling.
Pushing.
It can be seen in so many ways.
I don't know what love is,
I don't know what it looks like,

I don't know what it feels like.

September 20, 2022, 3:07 AM

More often than not, I pinch myself
I question whether I've died or if I am truly awake.
I wonder how moments like this exist.
It's usually little moments.
Moments with no significant value where I'll press
my nail to the skin on my finger,
And more often than not I feel it and then know,
That I am indeed alive.

September 28, 2022, 1:18 AM

I hate the way I love.
Because it's always the dominant,
Never the recessive gene.

September 28, 2022, 1:18 AM

The distaste in her eyes,
I never quite understood it.
Have him if you please,
But don't hate me for it.

October 23, 2022, 1:05 PM

If I die,

Don't mourn for me,

Celebrate me.
Please don't cry.
I couldn't bear the thought of leaving this earth
knowing it would break your heart.
It's okay to smile without me.
It's okay to laugh without me besides you.
It is okay to be a family without me in your arms.
It is okay to still love with me gone.
When I die,
As we all will,
Please don't cry too long.
I know you value my life,
And I do too,
But don't be too sad.
It'll break me,
That I cannot hold you,
That I cannot keep you safe and sound.
When I am dead,
Carry living your life as if it doesn't affect your
happiness that I'm gone.
I'll be there in your laughter.

October 24, 2022, 10:56 AM

I wonder sometimes,

If I'm the only one who misses you.
Am I,

The only one who stares at you.
I see our eyes flicker to each other, and I pass by
you waiting for them to meet yours.
I wonder,
Do you feel as deeply as do I?
Or do you just not meet me I to eye?

November 12, 2022, 2:50 PM
Sometimes I think if I should drive myself to insanity.
Would it really be so bad to give into obsession?
Would I finally then be satisfied?
Why do I like, feeling sick to my stomach?
Maybe it's a reminder,
That I can breathe.

November 12, 2022, 8:28 PM
I think I'll go first,
Since I haven't lost anyone yet.
I think I'll be the first one lost.

January 2, 2023, 11:47 PM
I cannot comprehend losing a loved one.
That's why I pray every night,
That I am taken away first.
Not because I don't value life,
But because,
I will never be strong enough to handle such grief.

January 3, 2023, 11:37 AM
This life is cruel, but I want to live.
I'd rather live in cruelty than die in solitude.

January 3, 2023, 11:38 AM
Playing takes the joy out of listening.
Creating takes the joy out of consuming.
It's a sad truth and a harder sacrifice.

January 3, 2023, 11:43 AM
It would be a waste to waste me.

January 9, 2023, 10:04 AM
Slice of my sword,
Blood drawn and courted.
Follow me,
And you shall see,
The demons waiting,
Below our beds,
Coming to get break through the surface,
Determined to screech,
At its impending doom.

January 9, 2023, 10:06 AM
I see you,
Drumming away,
Pattering at my heart.
Why can't you just leave me alone?
Tried once,

Failed twice,
Just go.

January 9, 2023, 6:43 PM

Sometimes it's too hard being my parents' child.

I'd rather not exist than deal with them and their scrutiny.

January 9, 2023, 6:52 PM

It's always "I'm your father" until you have to take responsibility.

January 9, 2023, 9:39 PM

I can no longer determine reality from delusion.
I'm hoping someone can save me from drowning.
Pinching myself has proven fruitless.
As the car glides down the freeway,
All I can envision is one another colliding.
Is any of this real?
Is any memory false?
Can life feel this real?
Can I still feel a pulse?
I'm inside my head, heart and brain
But am I living?
Or just in vain.

January 9, 2023, 10:11 PM

I love you,
I just don't say it.

January 16, 2023, 1:16 PM
Bells will ring when our eyes meet.
And water will fall from the heavens above us,
Showering us with love.
And in warmth I'll lock your eyes to my heart.
Turn the keys of our hands,
And run towards you,
Wondering when else we'll meet again.

January 27, 2023, 2:00 AM
My husband,
I pray every night God brings you to me.
My husband.

January 31, 2023, 8:18 PM
How can one not fall in love with her?

When she looks up at you with those eyes,
And trembling hands.
A plead in her sorrows,
And wisps in her hair.
How can one not fall in love with a woman such as her,
Such beauty and grace.
In the way she loathes about,
And those lips that damn me to hell.
How can I not fall in love with all her imperfections,
That I only see as perfections.
Mrs. Devine,

I'll like to call you Mrs. Mine.
How can one leave her behind?
I'll follow her through the bushes and thorns.
How could I not love her?
When I deeply love her eyes,
And when I hear her cries,
I crumble inside.

February 2, 2023, 8:06 AM
I notice now,
That my favorite songs are the ones I listen to the least,
Out of fear I'll ruin them,
And how they cannot be more different.
One speaks of losing passion and the death coming from it.
And the other speaks to not giving up on those passions.
It makes me think,
How often we find ourselves on two sides of the same coin,
And how when someone flips that coin, we cope with its outcome.

February 5, 2023, 11:59 AM
Is it childish to say I miss you and want to see you although I have never met you?

February 6, 2023, 10:17 AM

I look to your shadow and wonder,
That even without your features,
You still look magnificent.

February 10, 2023, 8:12 AM
Sometimes it upsets me the world can't hear the music I listen to.
But then again, not everyone has voices bouncing
around in their heads,
Making it impossible to sleep.

February 13, 2023, 10:13 PM
You must understand,
My cruelty,
Is what I think is best for me,
Even if it hurts you.
However,
It doesn't dispense from nowhere.
It only comes when you are cruel to me,
Then, and only then is mine justified.

February 13, 2023, 10:13 PM
You're everything I've ever wanted.
Being with you would be the dream,
But what happens when I wake up.
And stop sleeping.
What happens then?
I can't tell if the sacrifice of sleeping is worth the
pain of staying awake at night.

February 17, 2023, 11:45 AM
People will treat you horribly and complain when their actions put me in a bad mood.

February 19, 2023, 5:53 PM
Lurking don't break.
Where are we off to?
I feel like slowing,
Losing,
Frict-ing and fract-ing.
Bite my tongue,
Feel a fracture,
The bones,
Fleshy rips,
Only a fraction.

March 3, 2023, 11:09 PM
At a certain point my life stopped feeling like reality.
Just delusions and filthy dreams.
Not even a pinch,
A nail and the thread,
A peel of skin,
Pull back,
Could bring me to the brink,
Of sanity.
None of it,
Felt real.

March 9, 2023, 10:21 PM

I don't stare at the ceiling often enough to realize there's a whole world there waiting to be explored.

March 9, 2023, 11:34 PM

He looks so fucking pretty when he cries.
But I don't ever want to see tears sparkle in his eyes.
A pout to help him shut it down,
An inhale, to steady the heart.
Eyes big and brown,
Seeing him cry,
I'll take the part.

April 1, 2023, 12:34 AM

I awake from my dreams,
Where I kissed my lover,
Only to realize it's fake.
And there's no one,
Only impending doom.
I look at my country and I'm scared.
Bombs are falling in the cages of my mind,
From my birth,
I've been conditioned to fear for my life.
Shelter, intruder,
World war,
Roe V Wade,

ICWA overturn,
Trans bans.
I'd put a bullet in my mouth,
But for My family I could not.
I'm afraid of this world,
Maybe I'll lay in the streets tonight.
I'm tired,
Minnesota riots,
Covid,
250 years,
Fall of an empire,
Pluto In Aquarius,
Willow project.
The children of today and the children of tomorrow I ask for forgiveness.
You cannot live a decent life.
You cannot love whom you want.
You cannot breathe without being questioned first.
We must be thankful for our parents,
For living the youths, we deserved.
For dooming us with its plastic and their carelessness.
A luxury of freedom we cannot attain,
One we couldn't afford from the moments we were conceived.
We are the future,
The leaders they'd tell us,
To clean up their messes,
Only not to allow us into office.
Only to silence us,

Only to be surprised we grew the way we did.
Was it so surprising we are gay?
Angry?
Depressed?
So different from you?
So, stressed?
Unwilling to work so mundanely?
I fear I may not be able to fight,
That I have no hero in me,
When times of need come upon me.
I fear my life and losing it,
Ironic considering I try to end it so often.
Slipping from my lips, "kill myself".
I want to live,
Have normal college years,
But I know I can't.
I'll never leave this place.
All significant parts of my life that were so easy for
the elderly, will be different,
Have been.
High school: Covid.
Middle school: trump.
Elementary school: lockdown drills.
I'll live a life of wonders and pain,
With so much happening,
So overwhelming,
I could never fit it into one singular story.
So don't ask me,
How was it?
It was miserable.

With small moments of such happiness sprinkled within my days,
Such happiness I may as easily lose to the loneliness.
Fear.
Misery of it all.
I guess no one in history had it easy but why us?
Why were we conditioned to have it worse?
Can we not just be free from it all?

April 1, 2023, 12:37 AM
One of these days I'll convince myself of inception,
That none of this could be real.
I fear the day may come sooner than later,
Wait for me on the other end please.

April 5, 2023, 4:18 PM
If I could just kill myself for one day,
I could finally find some modicum of peace.
If I could only just freeze time just for one day,
I could finally think things through.
With no time to waste.
Of course I'd come back.
I wouldn't leave forever, just 24 hours.
But unfortunately, the world doesn't work like that.
So now I sit here,
Plagued in my anxiety,
Watching the minutes pass me by.

I try to forget my thoughts,
But they re-occur to torture me, forcing me to make decisions.
Oh, if only the world worked like that,
But if I did those things,
I wouldn't be able to come back.

April 10, 2023, 10:11 PM

I'll never get to see the world of tomorrow if I die today.
When I look at a person who took their life,
I say, "You never got to see how the world turned today",

And notice my reflection rippling back at me.

April 10, 2023, 11:13 PM

I thought it was behind me,
The thoughts,
The pleads,
Begging,
Churning feelings.
The high and chase of it all,
To perish,
To jump,
Looking for a way out.
I thought it was past me,
But I'm still searching,
Everyday,
For a way out.

April 12, 2023, 3:20 PM

If you can't tell I like you,
I can tell that you don't like me.
Because if you were only to look at me long enough,
You'd see me looking back at you.

April 19, 2023, 4:54 PM

Death is so weird,
I see pictures of him,
And in my head, all I think is,
He's dead! HE'S FUCKING DEAD! HE'S GONE!
HE'S NOT HERE! HE'S DEAD!
But he looks so happy in the pictures?
He looks so alive on my phone,
I don't understand what it means that he's dead.
What part of him looks inhumane?
He still looks pretty in the pictures,
It's not possible,
Why would he be dead?
It's such a waste for him to waste away.
People loved him,
So why,
Would he want to be dead?

May 1, 2023, 10:59 AM

I want to kill myself,

But I can't.
It's that simple.
I'm not rewarded such a luxury.
Little things can hurt me,
Sending me into a spiral,
But I can't excuse that as a way to hit the exit sign
on my way out.
Fuck it up,
Suck it up,
And just fucking live.

May 1, 2023, 11:11 AM
Can't I just forget it all?
It's gonna be okay,
It's gonna be so slay.
What's the worth in useless words?
And priceless pessimism?
What about pride?
What about the obliteration of optimism?
What a funny circle I find myself crawling into.
Could it get any worse?
Oh—could I?
What's the point of all these writings?
All my words,
Apologies!
I do know this is truly hard to read,
I just can't find any reason to continue writing.
My passions,
My ambitions,
Slip away,

Sippy cup,
Falling to the floor,
Look at me,
Disappointing the child within me.
Look at me,
The dreams I've splattered from my cup.
Put me down,
I'm fine,
Suicide watch has never really been my thing.
Repeat,
Repeat,
It's hard to listen to but the sounds hurt so good,
So, well.
My emotions feel fucked,
Jumbled up,
Running about.
Speak to me and I sound fine,
I'm burning up inside,
Ready to implode.
If someone says anything else to me,
Leave me alone,
I'd rather die alone.

May 1, 2023, 11:16 AM

Time ticks by,
But I don't remember getting here.
Do I look behind me and retrace where I've been or
who I was?
I'm lost in thought,

Feet moving before my mind.
My name doesn't stick on my tongue.
Was today a good day
Or a bad one?
If I don't remember, do I still have the choice on
what day it could turn to?

May 5, 2023, 1:31 PM

Today I've learned,
That each one of us are dying.
Every second we live,
We are also stepping closer to death.
The very thing I've feared,
The very thing I've prayed and desired,
Poured my heart out into these words,
And spiraled.
Dip, drain, drip
Has come true.
Every time I've lived, I've died.
Every time I've loved, I feel my heart stopping.
Every beating lullaby, and butterflies,
Have been emptied.
The string running short,
Road yellow and green,
I can't escape death.
So, what am I, supposed to just accept?
Even in my misery, I'm dying.
Even in my laughter, I'm dying.

I fear I mind find peace,
Modicum, pendulum,
Now knowing such truth,
And how it will act upon my desires,
And bid me farewell on bad days,
I have yet to see,
And soon to learn,
If it could save me.
Or make death all the more pleasurable,
Or life less.

May 6, 2023, 11:01 PM

I'm married to the moon,
For he is far away and sometimes likes to hide
behind the branches of trees.
Sometimes he's not all there,
But it doesn't infuriate me.
Sometimes I am not all there either,
And some days are dark,
But on the days, I do see him, he is shining
beautifully bright.
In front of me,
Talking to me about the sun and the stars.
I am married to the moon I say,
And everyone looks at me funny calling me mad,
But he loves it when I stare at him,
And when I talk about my dreams and desires to
him, he listens.
He only come out at night,
When no one else can see him.

When no one else can bother him and with the
branches of tress he hides,
And our love blossoms,
And no one can bother us,
For it is dark,
And the only light is him.
I am married to the moon, and I live in the fantasy
and that only I can see him and have him.

May 7, 2023, 6:38 PM

Here I go again,
Being scared of the future.
Fear of seeing my elderly mother,
Fear that one day I'll be nearing my last day.
Fear when my mother's joints begin to hurt.
I may shoot myself in the head,
Then deal with the pain that I am losing her.
That I am losing,
And there is nothing I can do to stop it from
happening.
That one day I'll rest in a chair as I await the casket
to be drawn of all that of those I love.
I know,
And I think everyone else does too,
That I am either first to be drawn closer to the
ground and the dirt,
Or the last fellow roaming about,
Waiting around for my turn,
While carving my name in the dirt.

May 7, 2023, 7:59 PM

Will you be with me when I go mad?
Will you take the gun from my hand whenever I point it at me?
Or will you let me weep?
Do you care enough about my happiness to let me lose my mind?
And sense of touch?
And sound?
Will you shield me from the pills I take each morning?
Or the lonesome hours I spend loathing?
Do you promise to make me grow old with you,
And find a reason to love,
And to live,
And to hold?

May 8, 2023, 10:35 AM

Why does no one get it!?
I have no goals in life!
I don't know what to do!!
I have nothing! I feel nothing!
Ands that's my normal.
What have I ever done to prove myself to you?
Why should I need to?
Can't I just exist?
I was made to breathe,
But you insist on smothering me.
Can't you just leave it to rest?

I'm not a child.
I'm not your little girl.
I am nothing.
Nobody,
And that's all I want to be,
Because then it means I'm just allowed to live.
If I have no label,
No meaning,
No love,
I can just live.

May 12, 2023, 10:38 AM
I think I may actually be insane,
Because I know just how to play everyone just right,
But I never use my power.
My brain,
For wealth,
It's so stupid.
The things I could get,
But no.
I use my power to kill myself.
Smile and laugh.
Say the right things while holding back too much.
If anyone could understand how easy it is,
I have almost enough for an overdose,
And could get the rest from the nurse.
I just have to move around some,
But my stupid mind won't let me,
Locking myself up so I can't hurt myself.

May 16, 2023, 11:42 AM
Every day I grow more tired of life.
I gain more and more reasons to end it.
When's gonna be my breaking point?
You? Or me? What will cause this downfall,
Ground less,
Madness.

June 19, 2023, 1:56 AM
He reminds me of hiding from the cold underneath my blanket.

August 3, 2023, 3:02 AM
He's got those eyes that just follow me around like the Mona Lisa.

September 1, 2023, 2:19 PM
I was kissed by a fairy.
A magical sprinkle of glitter on my head.
An irresistible candylike lips.
Pink, rosy cheeks.
She bent down and kissed me.
I never felt freer,
Better.
Come and please stay.
I can make a home up in the trees,
In the forest where you reside and live.
I'll follow you like a siren.
That fairy who kissed me,

Meaningless

On the day she could've missed me,
Wished me to be yours.

September 13, 2023, 9:16 AM
It is almost volatile when the teacher looks at my work and says nothing.

September 26, 2023, 4:48 PM
How are we even sure the future exists? The present exists, I feel this present. I know I exist in this moment alone but how are we so sure there is a future beyond this present time? How does time travel work? How are we so sure that there's this timeline that we're following and there's version of us living in the future? Is time, the future, only every inched forward by every going second instead of such timeline. Because if all of future exists, then what stops people from visiting us? Is it because the future doesn't actually exist in a whole? Is the past and present the only thing that is actually relevant and existing?

There Is no future timeline whatsoever, it's not possible that time would stretch that far and beyond and not circle back and reach us. Only the present exists as the time ticks by, not the future.

October 19, 2023, 12:04 AM
I ask you to capture the sky because I love it.
You set out to retrieve it the morning after,

Promising to hand it to me in my palms.

October 19, 2023, 12:10 AM
My heart jumps at the sound of his hands in my hair.
My nights fade away as he shines there.

October 19, 2023, 3:46 PM
My need for freedom is so strange and overwhelming.
I feel animated,
Like a character,
Wishing to fly high like a bird.
Maybe someday I'll be born again to fly and flee.
Glide the knife across my neck and slide through my throat.

November 11, 2023, 3:04 PM
I care not if someone works with me,
I stand for what I believe.
I am an artist,
I do not need someone else to tell me what to create.
I do need the permission of others to make something beautiful.

November 27, 2023, 8:12 AM
I don't remember a single part of my life where I was truly happy,
There was always something going on.

November 27, 2023, 11:34 AM
Some people are born as fighters,
And they're just that,
Fighters,
Soldiers,
Children obsessed with war even during peace.
Always hoping,
Silently wishing they could take charge and go to war.
And risk it all with nothing to lose.
I am unfortunate to say I may be one of those children.

November 30, 2023, 9:33 PM
I look at my old memories and think to myself,
Ahh, back when life was good.
But life was never good.
Back then I don't remember the pain,
And the sorrow,
Or the many, many times I tried to leave the earth,
Although fleeting, the thoughts that numbed my mind.
I only look and see a smile,
A pretty haircut,
Something to make me think I'd do it all over again.
But the truth is,
Nothing can be better than the present.

Even if life itself is horrible,
Nothing can be better than where we are now.
December 1, 2023, 5:41 PM
I sit and think,
How lucky I am to be an American.
The people dying everywhere,
But,
America makes us think this.
Waging war across the globe,
To make them seem victorious,
To make me foolishly think,
I'm so grateful.

December 3, 2023, 3:09 PM
Just because she's alive in your memories doesn't mean she's walking this earth.

December 3, 2023, 3:17 PM
I'm thinking, maybe the human mind wasn't made to process death,
In the ways a human can't stand the stench of rotten flesh,
Or the way it can be traumatic if you hurt another human.
But maybe it's just me,
And my stupidity.
Perhaps I am the only one,
Who doesn't understand what it means when someone is gone.
What does that make me?

Utterly alone?

December 10, 2023, 2:50 PM
You know what's sad and no one knew?
Days before my 18th birthday I wanted to kill myself,
Which is why it was so surreal I made to 18.
Days before graduation I attempted again.
I had to beg myself to stay,
Stay and watch the world around me change,
And leave everything behind and face my biggest fear,
Growing up.
The stress of being a teen exists and,
It's suffocating.
Looking back on the old days and wishing to relive them is a joke.
You wanted to die,
Now you don't.

December 10, 2023, 3:03 PM
What a strange funny thing,
I read these poems alongside you,
And my heart breaks.
I ask myself, who hurt you?
It's funny,
How even at the smallest inconvenience,
I'm more focused on living and what comes next,
And abandon the hole I'd been digging all these years to put myself in the dirt.

I have to get to class,
And eat,
And work on my projects.
I just have no time to die.
No thoughts of it even on my worst days.
I guess this is what they call living?
And growing?
College truly is different.
I seem happy.
I am alive,
And alone,
But not sad.
Penniless,
But I care not for it.
I'll count my change happily.
Who cares.
I am living!
Is this what it feels like?
To be mentally stable?
How very strange.
I hope I stay in this glitch forever.

December 10, 2023, 7:36 PM
I thought when I turned 18, I'd be 18 forever,
Then I turned 19.

December 24, 2023, 10:59 PM
I think you and I lived as one in previous lives.
I'm sorry I didn't love you more then,
But I'll find you,

And love you once again.

December 30, 2023, 1:27 AM
We fought,
We loved,
We lived a life in each other's arms up until the very end.
That's how I want our story to be told,
When it ends,
When one of us goes,
And the other is asked to recall what it was.
We spent a lifetime together.
And I can't wait to see you again in the future,
When I go.

December 30, 2023, 1:32 AM
I want to stay here all night cuddled up beside you like it's our last night on earth.

January 10, 2024, 3:16 PM
I'm a different person in front of the mirror.
I talk and talk,
And smile and dance.
Laugh out loud.
I am free,
But with people,
I am like a mouse.
Silent,

Tiny,
Trapped.

January 12, 2024, 1:13 AM

I'm crazy to think I have this chance with you.
When I see you,
In pictures and videos,
Although I can't touch you,
I wish too.
I close my eyes and dream.
I'm so lost in those dreams,
Believing we could be.
We haven't met,
And if we did how could I explain it?
I dreamt of us?
I'm crazy.
I think I might just be insane,
To feel so much love for someone I can only see on my screen.
Oh, to be in your life,
Must be obsession to feel this way,
Wanting to get close,
Not wanting to seem crazy,
Knowing all about your life,
But knowing none of me.
My man,
My man,
My lady,
I dream and dream in my fantasy about you.
What a craze.

What an obsession.
Put you on a pedestal.
A mere human am I,
I lurk beneath the stars.
An idol and her fan,
What a world I've come to live in.

January 12, 2023, 1:22 AM
I'm trapped inside my head,
Constantly dreaming.
I notice now only,
That you weren't real,
Just an illusion I had loved in my mind,
Just a version I had created to love me,
And make me feel less lonely.
I wash away the thoughts.
The life I'd built in this world.
The dreams I'd dreamt.
The conversations we had.
You are real, just not mine.
Driving myself to delusion thinking that is the only
way to live,
To love,
To succeed.
Follow your heart but I forget what it wants.
I'm set on having you,
The unattainable.
Oh, I ask the Universe to bring us together.
If it is fate let it be fated,

Because I feel so hard in love for someone, I'd never know.
I could travel across the seas,
To the ends of the world,
And still not find you there,
Holding me.
The life I had wished,
The dreams I had lived in,
The things I use to cope.
Wake up now silly dear.
The real world is cold and damp,
But you must live it.
Say goodbye to the dreams,
And say no, though you love it.

January 12, 2024, 12:14 PM
I fell in love with someone with your body and your face,
But you only existed in my mind.
Every time I see you,
I'm reminded of heartbreak,
But you don't know me,
And somehow, it's easier to cope that way.
I was alone when it started,
And I'll be alone when it ends.

January 22, 2024, 2:57 PM
The more unconventional I am, the happier I am.
The happier, brighter my soul shines.
It took me 18 years to learn,

And when I finally said it,
Something within me felt free.

January 22, 2024, 3:03 PM
The warmth of your body is the only thing keeping me going.
When it ceases to exist,
Will I?

January 29, 2024, 1:32 PM
I think maybe I might be wasting my youth away,
Because I'm not in love with calamity,
With chaos and danger.
Although a deep rage within me bubbles, I feel as though I'm adulting wrong or too quick.
I'd rather be peaceful,
Stay home instead of party,
Keep to myself instead of date,
But maybe I'm just protecting myself.
Keeping myself away from being truly free.
Dilute these rules and rhythms,
I shouldn't have my life figured out,
Peace just yet,
I am youthful so be youthful.
I have until my 30's,
I have my whole life to be peaceful.

January 30, 2024, 6:18 PM
Our instinct avoidance of other humans,

star candy

I've seen it as children,
Stepping onto the bus,
Each kid avoiding the other one seat to themselves.
College students,
Seated every other chair to avoid sitting next to one another.
Adults on the train seeking empty seats than to occupy one next to another.
Why?
Humans themselves hate one other and we suspect why Mother Nature rejects us.

February 1, 2024, 8:04 AM
I hope my friends suffer the guilt of 30,000 people. They chose not to speak up when they had every right, reason, and free will too, because it was "too political," "not my war" "I'm not educated enough". I hope you can say that to a child who was orphaned. A man who dug with his bare hands in the rubble. A mother who miscarried. All the people who suffered. They weren't numbers but you seemed to care more about the other sides. All lives matters but the one currently being lost, right? Can you explain in the future and don't lie, I won't forget, I won't let you either. Your complacency spoke volumes within me. My dearest friends, fuck you. I was too cowardice to fight you and stand tall, but I could not continue in my morals to love you. Have nice lives, delete my number, and free

falestine, for all time and forever. May no one
bother you for the next 1,000 years.

February 4, 2024, 11:01 PM
Society is a man-made concept meant to torture us.

February 7, 2024, 10:06 PM
His eyes were saying I can't live without him, but his mouth was quivering uncontrollably.
All I respond was "I know."
And he cried some more.

February 7, 2024, 10:43 PM
He was like a desert rose,
As soon as I saw him, part of me wanted him and wanted to protect him.
His profound beauty overtook me and my very being from the first moment I laid eyes on him.

February 8, 2024, 8:43 AM
I don't ever want to leave this world,
When its beauty is so serene and pure.
How could I look away?

February 8, 2024, 8:45 AM
Why do we call it dystopian?
It's not even a reflection of our humanity, or our time,
It's our present.

We push back our unpleasantries of today by calling
it dystopian.
No, it's just reality,
And call it so.
Those in power care not for us,
But the greens in their overstuffed pockets.
Call it as it is.
Say it with your voice,
And let everyone hear you.
Our reality is fucked.
We live in the end times.
Hold the ones you love,
It's going to get bad.

February 9, 2024, 7:59 PM
Feel so underdressed.
Words flying against my skull,
Music in my ears.
I'm typing away asking where you're at?
You're late,
I'm the corner,
Sitting by myself the whole table for myself.
Guess I should order.
In a dress that's too tight on my body,
My stomach not flat enough to hide its shape.
I look all around watching the door waiting, For a
face I know to pop up and come through.
I wish,
I need more friends,
I need more brown ones.

Meaningless

I feel so white here,
In this room with people my own shade,
I feel so bleak.
But parts of me is still smiling,
Watching the people having fun,
I don't mind being alone.
I'm just putting on a front of anxiety to hide the fact
I'm completely fine being all alone. But I know it
seems weird, so I'll be anxious instead.
I'll bite my inner lip,
I'll press on my knuckles to pop them,
I'll stare off,
Type at my phone,
Check the time but truly it makes no difference.
I think I'm fine with it and the weird stares.
I think I look cute.
I'll be seated with someone I don't know,
Maybe I'll open my mouth to say something,
Maybe I won't who knows.
Oh well,
I'll go to call you and hear that same voicemail,
Or you'll hang up when you pick up,
Always late.
I sit here waiting,
And I've gotten used to the tightness around my
curves and watching others look pretty,
Hoping to walk up to them and talk.
What do you call that?
Loneliness?
Delusion?

Should I not be furious?
I sit here and wait,
My back begins to hurt as I curl over the table.
The joints in my neck feeling heavy as I stare down at my phone wanting to look up and just observe hoping someone was observing me too.
I'll listen to romantic music to make myself, wish someone were watching me.
Someone was craving me and deciding indefinitely that they needed me and only me and we'll see who does.

February 9, 2024, 8:14 PM
Been here an hour disappointed at every look to the door where I don't see you.

February 9, 2024, 8:45 PM
I just went home crying,
All dolled up with no destination to go.

February 11, 2024, 2:16 AM
Love fucks me up so much because it just brings me back to my dreams.
Deep down I know I shouldn't sleepwalk,
But when I'm with you, I can't help but close my eyes when loneliness overtakes me, and I need a friend.
I need a narrative.
I need someone to love me even if it's not real.

I always say I'm a writer,
I just didn't realize all I was doing was writing in
my head.

February 13, 2024, 12:44 PM
**When people do not understand sarcasm my
heart cries.**

February 13, 2024, 8:16 PM
He looked for her in every woman until I met him
I saw that sadness overtake him once again,
I hadn't noticed he'd been pouring his heart out until
the vase had shattered,
Taken out from under him and all of him was
pouring out for us to see.

February 14, 2024, 1:11 PM
I don't get the desire to live,
It's all so confusing,
Our timelines skewing.
Am I to be old and resentful too?
Is this the cycle I will also go through?
The youth is youth,
The youth throw themselves into life and
experience,
Old hate them.
It keeps turning and turning this way, everyone is
always afraid of us.

In every generation, in all of life, they've always
been afraid of us,
As if they don't grow up like this.
Life changes too fast in only ten years.
Only when I take my timeline out of a larger picture,
Solitude and alone,
Can I make sense of life,
And love it.

February 14, 2024, 3:05 PM
**Turn your back to the wind, it's stronger than
you think,**
It's the front of us really, that is weak.

February 14, 2024, 3:11 PM
Panic overtook me as I searched my pockets.
Would panic overtake me if I lost myself too?

February 28, 2024, 9:57 AM
What has the world come to we ask.
We don't not realize the world has always been so
cruel.
Only nature,
Unmade,
Not touched and deprived from man can be
beautiful.
We have always been at war,
Sudan,
Congo,

Palestine,
You deserve so much more than I could give but no one shall dare to forget the way you've suffered.

March 3, 2024, 2:12 PM
People are so beautiful.
I sit and eat,
The wind is so light and feathery,
I am content,
Calm.
I rarely find time to be calm nowadays.
The city is so beautiful in the early days of spring.
How can one possible despise life in moments like these?

March 22, 2024, 12:25 AM
I sometimes think the moon is my best friend,
Consistent,
Changing,
Hidden but never truly gone.
And on the brightest nights,
You look at me and I look back,
Unable to tear eyes away to say hi,
Hello,
How have you been since we've last spoken?
How does the sun treat your burns?
How is life treating me on land,
A reassuring glow.
On my sickest days,
You come out to say I'm here! I'm here!

On the stariest nights,
On the ones with no lights,
We look at each other,
Such an understanding in our gazes,
A glow in our eyes,
Like we know incredibly well,
Without speaking,
What the other has been up to.
Naughty and nice,
I am able to speak freely with you.
My best friend,
You shine!
Such a magnificent glow!
Shine down on me always,
And I look up to you every time I see you.

March 22, 2024, 6:48 PM
As a woman,
We are never truly allowed to exist fully.
A man is never scrutinized for existing simultaneously as bad and good.
He can be a good friend and a horrible father,
And abuser and a best man,
Charming and gentle to some but horrific to another.
Women are never allowed to exist that fully.
As human beings it is silly to put ourselves into these boxes,
And bottle all our complexities.
We can be billions of things at once at any given moment.

Meaningless

I can be mean to someone and kind to another.
Does that make me a bitch or a lover?
Women are not allowed to be that complex,
They are not allowed to be bad at something and good at another.
They are collectively bad at everything,
Unintelligence, un-funny, too fat, too ugly.
Women cannot exist,
And we fight amongst ourselves to argue what womanhood is or what it is not.
We fight to identify what is means and what it cannot be without realizing it can be both.
It can be about babies and pink, about assault and laughter, drinking and sex, sobriety and class, work and motherhood.
A woman in this society is not allowed to be anything but washed up or washed up.
Men are allowed to be everything.
Never scrutinized for existing, for their sex, for their accomplishments,
But women must either enjoy it or forbid it.
We fight,
And some have forgotten,
We fight to exist, in fullness, in the complexity of our beings.
Womanhood is not just about pink,
But it's not, not about it.
It can be whatever I need it to be whatever I desire it to be to be.
We as women are complex.

We must remember we are fighting to keep our complexity,
And show that we deserve to exist just for the reason that we do.

March 28, 2024, 5:56 PM
Can you see me too?
From the window,
Reflective glass,
Smile!
You're on camera.

March 28, 2024, 6:05 PM
As happiness alludes me it has become decidedly more difficult to get up in the mornings, finding wills underneath my fingernails.
Burrows deep beneath my pillow.
A will to swallow,
A pill to escape my mind scape.
Where is my will?
In the palms of my hands,
It is scratchy,
Dry, a landscape, an atmosphere.
Plants growing green from my ears.
I searched blindly.
Eyes blackened and shut.
Skin peeling over my wounds.
Suddenly it entraps my mouth.
How strange?
Where is the will?

Meaningless

Where is the life,
In the gloomiest of days and night?
A raindrop alone could dissipate me entirely.
I do not recognize,
The own face I wear.
Could I wear yours instead?
Reach over and yank it from your body,
I desire it more,
I need it more,
No one can know.
What hides beneath me.
Silk sheets,
My skin chafes,
What excites me now?
No more,
School?
Cake?
Drawing?
I would place a black line on black paper,
So, you could see how clearly, I'd disappear
amongst the crowd.
Figure you know me better than I?
Do you!
I am unsure of what I become now.
Whomst I am supposed to be in this time?
My dreams say something other than I am,
How am I to reach you?
Up in the sky all alone?
My dreams must be so lonely,
I am not there to live you,

My apologies,
I am just feeling weak.

March 28, 2024, 6:05 PM
**My bad, the sky cleared up, ignore my last post.
Lol.**

March 28, 2024, 6:09 PM
The more I live the more I've noticed life truly is a spectacle. What is the point of trying? What is the point of dying? Can one make sense of it all? Is it good or bad that it exists within me?

March 28, 2024, 6:13 PM
Is it so unfair we do not get another chance at this life thing.
Can't I just die and respon?
Can I not just take a break from it and resurrect?
What makes me so un-special I do not get favored by God?
What an annoying concept,
It means I must try,
Must find a purpose.
Cannot I just be lazy? And free? And rich?
Must I also exhaust myself and dream?
Scrounge for a penny,
Fall in love too early I have not met my person yet and wait,
Must I be amazing?

Can I not just get to the good part!

March 28, 2024, 6:17 PM
I have a common concept that death is swift and painless, but it is not.
It is suffering,
Death is suffering,
No one goes easily.
Your body fights to keep you alive long after your mind has given up.
The inner workings of your body enage to keep you alive.
Do it a favor and make it easier for them to do their jobs and just live,
Damn you.

March 30, 2024, 2:53 PM
I realize no matter how old I am,
I am still a girl sitting in my bed,
Dreaming of a fairytale marriage.

April 7, 2024, 7:00 PM
I miss the clouds,
The sky is blue and lightness.
I miss their presence.

April 8, 2024, 2:58 PM
My moon you had passed over the sun and I had not seen you,

How bright you shone.

April 9, 2024, 7:37 PM
It's so weird to be,
Muslim growing up and being grown in America.
You feel uncomfortable and out of touch in your own spaces, amongst your own people.
It can be such a horrifically alienating experience.
I've never felt comfortable being Muslim around Muslims in America.
I was never Muslim enough.
I never knew anyone or connected in the way my cousins in Pakistan did community was and as foreign as my skin a concept I cannot comprehend.
It's a part of my identity I never feel whole enough in,
But I can't seem to let it go,
It's all I've ever known.

April 9, 2024, 7:39 PM
Eid has always been fun,
But I find myself marveling at the women,
And their beauty,
It is my gayest moments I fear,
Hijabi's are so pretty.

April 10, 2024, 10:17 AM
He burns just like my favorite drink,
He's insatiable.

Meaningless

April 15, 2024, 10:52 AM
I don't want to live on earth anymore,
I'd rather live on mars.
Maybe travel and meet Pluto,
Tell her I don't think she's too small,
Tell her she's still in my orbit.
I still pay attention to her still and see her,
Maybe I,
Wonder if I'm truly tired of this world,
Or just this World.
Could living with Pluto help me heal?
Alone at last,
Bored at last,
Away from the crazies,
How peaceful you must be.
Sadness overtook you first when they told you were not enough,
But now you must find solace in the peace, yes?
Oh, how I wonder to meet you,
Perhaps Pluto you, the moon and I could just get away from it all and relax.
No one to speak to unless ourselves,
No one to distract from the calmness,
Create a new orbit with me and travel the worlds.
The darkened sky, miles and light years, always and find a quiet spot near a black hole, who knows he could be in need of company too, just hope he would not swallow us, and rest.
We can throw asteroids to and frow,

Play catch,
We could orbit one another,
Just us, no other celestial beings.
No words need be exchanged we could look and understand,
Live in harmony,
No humans.
Wouldn't that be nice?
Just me, Pluto, and the Moon,
A few stars sprinkle the skyline how beautiful.
I'd never have to worry about anything else.

April 18, 2024, 6:05 PM
How can you be so sure you love me?
How are you sure?
I am not in love with another. If I were to be set up, arranged and shipped off I would never fall in love with another.
So, I do not have to worry of his feelings nor mine.
It would just be a companionship.
Marriage of convivence at best.
But you, you change everything. If we were to marry, I would not, I could not let go.
So yes, I'll question your integrity, how can you be so sure you can love me and be with me for the rest of your lives because if we are to marry, I won't let go.
I'd rather die, I'd rather marry someone else than let you go.
So, are you sure?

Can, you be sure?
Reassure me at last.

May 3, 2024, 8:18 PM
My mother once told me about the baby she had that did not make it in this world,
And I am once again reminded ever so often of this story.
How different my life would have been with one more brother.
I image him to be witty and kind,
Tall and caring,
I image us as close.
Whenever I think back to that baby, I mourn.
A piece of me feels missing.
I mourn a man,
A child,
A baby,
A Brother,
I had yet to know.
I wonder what you could've been named,
What you could've looked like,
What you could've liked,
And I am glad now,
Of the siblings I do have and gotten the blessings to know.
But I still wish I could've known you,
It's a shame we lost you big brother.

May 3, 2024, 8:45 PM
It brings me great comfort and great anger that society has remained as it has since it's dawn.

May 3, 2024, 8:46 PM
To know I am not the only queer in my lineage, and how alone they must have felt, breaks my heart in two.
Even now years later, I've yet to be accepted by all.

May 3, 2024, 8:46 PM
Beauty itself cannot comprehend you,
Cannot even contain your name,
That face,
Body and mind.

May 11, 2024, 7:12 PM
I want to forget everything,
I know it is selfish,
I want my old life back.
One of bliss and not constant blues,
I do not want to see,
So, I look away.
I know they want it too,
Their pain is much bigger than mine,
But I find myself becoming bitter.
Everyone needs fucking help,
And it's not their fault they cannot stand,
This whole world and its finances crumble.

Meaningless

I too, struggle with money.
Why should I donate to you and your family?
Asking the poor to fix the poor.
Fuck the rich,
Cut them into bits and feed yourselves,
Until bellies are full once more.
Why must I care?
Mustn't look away.
Must feel guilty within my privilege.
I am sorry,
Truly.
My soft organs are sorry still,
I cannot help at all.
I feel myself getting sick.
Maybe it is the human flesh I digest.
I crave to divest,
I must retain my sanity, but I find myself in bed.
Sick in the head I lay,
Unable to help a single soul,
Crying, crying.
You deserve more,
But I am tired of hearing of your pain,
I struggle at your level.
I can never understand what it means to live through this war,
But the war in the head is steadfast and strong.
Forgive me my selfishness, I must retain my sympathy.
Compassion of the human heart,
If it were myself, I'd be frustrated too.

I'd spit down on those looking away,
But I look to myself broken as before,
Torn at the simplicity of my privilege to turn away.
No Human mind can comprehend such horror,
Not yours in the field,
Nor mine from my home.
You are not at war,
You are being slaughtered,
I am sorry my dears for my weakness.
The bitter taste of flesh and blood spewing from my mouth.
Here take, my soul,
Take everything, I own,
But please stop asking for my help.
My dear please stop weighing on my shoulders.
Why must I be the only one to listen?
I can't seem to help myself.
How must I help thee?
Those who look to me?
Look like me?
With my name you bear,
I see you martyred instead of free,
Take my flesh,
My skin and bones,
I feel as if it's all I have left to give.
I selfishly hide my money,
I'm saving it I say!
And use it to expense to pamper myself.
I use it in guilt to donate,

Meaningless

Trying to see if it washes my sins and makes me feel better.
I have the right to save money, yes?
In a genocide do I have the right of luxury?
Is it not matter enough I care?
I fight? I shout? I donate?
Someone, tell me I've done enough.
Someone, tell me I'm doing enough.
I fear I have to do more,
I feel the burden as I am the only one to listen.
I see your donations unfulfilled what am I to do?
Is no one else awake?
You bourgeois,
You fuckers sitting in your money,
Give it,
Do something with it!
The poor, the dying, the struggling, forced to help the slaughtered.
Wear your pretty dresses,
Don't blame us for ripping them off you.
I blame my table manners,
My inability to let things go,
I have never been rich,
The sight of money makes me flounder.
I cannot so easily give it up or I will have nothing,
But they too have nothing.
Forced to beg for someone to find it reason enough to let them live.
My dearest individuals,
Held in concentration,

The world owes you more than you could ever
pocket,
Souls than you could ever bury,
Foods that you could choke on,
Love to your fullest extent.
You deserve freedom and your homes.
You deserve divestment and support.
This world is cruel and lawless,
But you did not ask to be in it.

May 11, 2024, 11:37 PM
I don't care! I don't care anymore!
I yell,
Hands over my ears like a child,
And yet only my heart can hear.
The instilled beliefs in me scream,
How American of me,
To peoples suffering.
To see people begging for help does not break my
heart now but inconveniences me more.
I feel as if no one can hear me,
I don't care!
I want to not care for you, but I'm forced to.
I used to think I had enough fire in my lungs to rebel
endlessly, but I realize now spending 7 months of
my life dedicated to such,
I do not.
My fire thins out,
Wispy flames,
And headaches.

Meaningless

Dead bodies and sighs,
I can't take it.
Why must everyone need something?
Climate change,
Floods,
War,
Genocide,
What the fuck am I to do?
I am tired and bitter,
And my anger misplaced.
My friendships suffer greatly at my hands.
Politicians still smiling as I attack those innocents.
Silence is complicit,
I'm fucking tired.
Let karma take you,
I care not to fight you.
I am sour and resentful,
Don't forget! Don't forget!
Just let me fucking forget it all!
Let me live in my bubble,
Selfish feelings covering me in a thin wrap.
It must be hard to live in your environment I understand,
You must be tired too,
I understand.
In the rain,
How will my fire spark?
May I have a moment to me?
I wish I did not feel such things,
I do not know what this makes me,

Morally am I wrong?
A bad person altogether?
I've lost all hope, wandering alone,
Even my shouts don't echo.
A rebellion fueled by hatred,
I've now misdirected it towards those in need themselves.
Those I'd sworn to protect and support,
Piss me off more than the arrogant fucks who chose to ignore it.
They're telling me not to look away,
And look at the horrific sights of bodies crumbled,
Stuck in bags,
Hanging off buildings,
No human mind,
Even a privileged one like mine can handle such sights and walk away un-fucked.
Children cut open,
Limbs spewed off,
Blood dripping from broken chins.
I apologize but I must look away at times.
You don't deserve to experience this either,
I feel so guilty for every move I make.
I can't take a second to myself,
I can't be selfish,
But I want to,
God knows I need to.

May 15, 2024, 12:53 AM

The way people react under pressure is so strange and weird.
I for one find myself laughing or making the most of it,
Call it an adventure.
Our car breaks down in New York City and we live 3 hours away.
Stay awake until 3 am and get home around 7.
I, for one run around in the airport not a care in the world,
Or walk outside in the rain at three in the morning.
I'll take the Uber or the train,
And now I don't know if it's gentlemanly or not,
The way my brothers react in the same situation,
Serious faces,
Anxiety pouring from their crevices.
The worried look in their faces and,
Bodies,
I wonder why.
Must you be such an ass? In a situation as such,
Why must you be so serious now?
Can we not call it an unfortunate adventure?

May 21, 2024, 8:41 AM
I hate working,
But I've finally grown to understand,
Why people fall into the ridiculous notion of constant slaving away.
Being an adult,
Is plain boring.

The need to grow,
The desire to be old and have your freedoms,
Gets overwhelmed by too much,
Too soon.
I find myself utterly bored beyond belief,
Besides schooling,
I find myself cramming to do something with my
life besides sitting around watching tv.
I work,
I shop,
I watch tv,
I am,
Bored.
I need sustenance,
I need something filling.
I find myself with too much time on my hands,
Forced to make something of myself.
I am not sure whether to be grateful,
Whether to take the opportunity or not.
I either sit in misery,
Or get up.
Both requires so much of my energy.
May 25, 2024, 4:46 PM

What am I to contribute to society now that I have money?
Does money = power?
Does power = influence?
If I have influence, do I use it for good?
What happens if I use it for bad?
What will you do now haven given me your money,

When I turn my back and spit something vile.
Am I to stay silent with my money?
Pay my bills and make my bed,
I am just a girl am I not?
In my twenties like you too bearing down on me,
Must I lie in my bed?
Now with money,
With my views,
What did I contribute to society to get so lucky?
Is it not karma of yours for believing in me?
Giving me so much as I have such little to you.
Is it not abusive,
To give such love,
Such interest in a being,
You fail to see they are not godly as you make them
a celebrity.
Who is to know what their heart holds until tragedy
unfolds.
Must I reveal to you your deceit!
What shall I do with mine?
Swallow it full and keep it down,
I pick my own sheets,
Fluff my own pillows,
Who is to tell if I am truly wicked or not?
Sorrows, sorrows,
You may keep your prayers,
Continue to uphold such values and make us all into
monsters,
Mold me into clay and mush,
And call it M. Rutt.

Beat me down senselessly,
When I lose my way and make a fool of myself.
You can call me Peeta,
I'll call me a mutt.
Is it not the utmost karma to create a celebrity?
Influence and power,
For the disappointment and deceit.
When the gluttony takes over their wallets,
And they chose not to mind such things like the suffering of our lower class.
Such a divide the middle class needs a lengthy glass to see the life beholding them behind a flask and the sewer trash.
If I were to be famous, would I falter too in my values?
Would my morals mean nothing?
I tell you know my audience,
If you are to like me,
Listen to me,
Adore and admire me,
Or hold such distaste for me.
Remember I too am human,
But I would never be so disgustingly distasteful to care not for those dying at the expense of my govern.

May 25, 2024, 4:49 PM
A complex contradictory,
I fear I've found my calling.
I am to be loud,

Meaningless

Full of laughter and light.
A confidence and sexuality,
A girl.
But am I not,
In need of quiet and space?
Moody and pessimistic?
Doubtful and solitary?
I should be allowed to both no?
But it does not make sense,
Or easier not knowing why I desire all sides of each coin.
Each emotion,
Each through and action,
Would ignorance really be a bad color on me?
Is it not better and less painful if I were to be stupid and simple?
Goodness, I wish.
I wouldn't overthink.

May 25, 2024, 5:13 PM
Must I always write of my despair?
Goodness, I read back all these words,
And notice just how dark my mind can be.
Goofy bitch sitting here and sad,
Oh baby,
Oh baby,
Get up off your ass.

May 26, 2024, 9:53 PM

A beheaded child,
It's my brother 's,
Blood in my backpack.
Legs mangled,
And burnt alive while sleeping.
You bomb our tents,
Piercing our hearts and igniting flames amongst a grieving people.
Fuck you!
I hope for you not to be real,
I can't stand this despair.
They do not deserve this deprivation,
And decapitation.
Children aged not 1,
Limp in my arms,
Piled into plastic bags.
I fear the effects of this horror on your minds and generations to come.
You nazis,
You scum,
You must suffer this shame.
This peace a non,
Residing in tents,
You still think to bomb us.
With nothing left to give to grieve,
You curse us.
My hollo heart.
Never forget,
Forget you too.
Criminals of war,

Rafah will be free.
Cost me my leg and my arm,
Take my heart and my head.
Carry me all with no soul left in my skin,
We will be free,
They shall be free.

May 29, 2024, 2:34 PM
Q me?
Who me?
Touch me,
Tease me,
Oh, screw you!
Sons of bitches who'll never let me be free!
I need my buddy,
I'm incomplete,
Call us Q and A-my.
You bitches can't compete,
Who you know, me?
Can't hear a beat,
Without a treat,
My hearts gots heat.
Feel me coldly,
Glide down the street,
Can't catch this feat.
Might as well try running on my feet.
My dear, oh deer,
Caresses me softly.
Who me?
Q me?

Sleep easily,
Try measly,
You weasel!
Fuck out of my way I can't stand this creat-
Urgently seek out a good man to follow suit.
Watch your way out, beware his boot.
Who?
Sucker!
Q-Tip.
Q-Phill.
Q-fell.
Do tell?
Que heh?
Leave say!
Sigh may!

May 29, 2024, 5:03 PM
I love being looked at and marveled,
But I don't like being harassed by men who stay ignorant and entitled.

May 30, 2024, 10:52 AM
I'm becoming more comfortable in my filth.
I don't know if that's good or bad.
My compulsiveness to stay clean deteriorates when I remind myself, "I'll take a shower tonight",
Allowing me to relax.

May 31, 2024, 5:25 PM
I've always been a fighter.
I've always been addicted to a war I was never born
into but dreamed of fighting,
Demanded of having.
Does that mean I have rage?
Unadulterated rage,
Generational rage I still need to get off my chest.
I find myself craving survival and violence.
I think I'd be a leader in war,
I'd be soldier,
I'd wish.
To command to scream out,
Maybe I just remain fearful,
Fearful I could lose everything and everyone I'd
ever known and what it may do to me.
Would I too be a jinx?
Or fall apart like powder,
Slipping sand through my fingers?

June 14, 2024, 1:37 PM
I want to love the way singers sing,
Poets write,
Artists paint their beloved.
Oh goodness,
My heart is so full.
Oh my,
Heart is so empty,
Waiting for you to set yourself into it.

Love them until the day I turn cold and blue and beyond.
In the 7 minutes left of my conscious I want to only think of you,
Until the last beat of my wretched heart,
Be just for you.
Come my way,
I sit and wait.
Dreaming and dreaming kicking my feet.
Wanting to kiss someone's lips,
Anyone's,
Please just anyone's at this point.
All I can do is think and think away unable to reach the real world in fantasy.
Craving beyond words and feelings for a love to feel secure in,
A warmth in my bitter cold chest,
I write of romance of fantasy,
With none in my life to recollect memories from.
I write too much,
So much,
But paper never meets my pen.
I'm lost in my mind scape,
I've lost the maze, haven't I?
How silly?
Yes!
Oh delusion,
Oh delusion,
How I wish to rid you from my being but cannot help falter, back into,

Meaningless

Your arms.
What if I spend my entire life here?
Buried in my own head,
Unable to love a real human besides the image mist
I've made in my mind?
Besides my dream,
My writing,
My pen shall be my downfall.
My mind,
A luxury I have yet to understand.
What if my body is too poor to afford my mind?
What happens to me?
Do I disintegrate away?
The unlocked knowledge and expertise,
The creativity and wisdom,
Sitting in my brain waiting to be opened.
How must I unlock you?
Should I sit in sanity behind the door or in the room?
Which is less painful?
Am I to have the ability to choose after I've seen
both sides.
After I've truly become me,
Become one,
Am I allowed to turn back in fear?
After I've unlocked my abilities, and greatness can I
crumble away and diminish?
I am afraid,
Someone take my fear away.
Do I crave human affection because I am afraid of
myself,

Being myself?
I need someone to distract me and reassure me.
What if I were to sit with myself and unlock me,
What happens then?

June 14, 2024, 1:53 PM
All these secrets I seem to hold,
Call me a liar!
All these references no one but me would understand.
Even my closest friends,
I fear you do not know me.
I hide,
Under my pen,
Under my secretes hoping one day keeping them will give me some rewards.
What meddles do I get for being deceitful?
Hiding my passions and personality.
Every connection I've made feels surreal,
Surface level and false.
It's easier to be honest with those I am not closest too.
Why does each friend of mine know me differently?
Get a different color from my rainbow,
The other side of each coin,
Extroverted and loud,
Hard and tough,
And soft and quiet, what am I truly?
What do my dearest friends think?
I do not even know myself,

And yet I know myself so deeply I fear no one else
can understand the way I do.

June 14, 2024, 2:02 PM
The insanity when realization hits,
That my dreams and delusions are fairytales taken
straight from the movies.
Wanda,
You and I are the same sitting here dreaming of a
man and family that is so unreal it drives you insane
you cannot have I must truly be insane.
But perhaps calamity is what I need to be free but
goodness I am sick in the head.
I am sick of being sick,
Can I not just leave these dreams alone forget they
existed and move on?

June 14, 2024, 2:10 PM
I can say I am proud,
I have begun taking pills.
My anxiety subsided,
And I have not abused my power once.
I have stayed responsible and not have tried to
overdose!
Not thoughts of ending my life crosses my mind or
plagues me frozen in my step.
Even in my boredom,
I have found myself back in the glitch,

I resort of filling my time with life rather than ending it.
How many times will I fall in and out of this glitch I do not know.
Years ago, if I told myself I'd be so responsible around pills,
And not tried to kill myself,
I don't know who'd I'd believe.
The crazy thought crosses my mind and yet I snort,
Oh well I hope this lasts longer than the last glitch.
Maybe it is the sunny weather,
Even though there is not much to look forwards to day to day to make me stay,
I still find myself not minding and not thinking of ending life,
And that is my bar,
I hope I don't succumb to the weight.
I will try my hardest, I like being happy,
And although I'm not always happy,
It's nice to not think about suicide.

June 17, 2024, 6:41 PM
I shall build an empire,
I will build my success.
My riches,
My gloom be gone,
I am exactly who I want to be.

June 22, 2024, 1:18 PM
I write my wedding vows,

With no one at the alter but me.

June 26, 2024, 1:17 PM
I'm afraid,
I might be a lesbian.
And accepting that is fearful but freeing,
And denying it is soul crushing but what society wants from me.
I cannot tell,
Who I am anymore.

June 29, 2024, 2:17 PM
Man fuck this fascists world!
Our state built on the backs of slaves,
Fuck you and all your rules.
Two Zionists running for president,
Put a bullet between 4 eyes and call it a day.
The land of freedom, land of opportunity,
Are we not Americans?
Arm ourselves,
Pluck out or finest guns,
And fucking kill those sons of bitches in power, why don't we?
As if we have no power,
As if the people have no rule,
Tell me is this not America?!
Built off violence,
Making homelessness illegal,
Is this not America?
Are we only to assassinate those who do any good?

Fuck,
Our history is built off of dead presidents,
So please,
Someone do me the fucking honor and take care of the fascists.
Someone please offer themselves and get their hands dirty and take out the Supreme Court and candidates.
Someone do something!
In times like this I fear this violence is the only answer,
I'm sick and tired of watching innocent peoples be killed.
Those who look like me,
Harbor my DNA,
And my names,
Sudanese,
Palestinians,
Congolese,
My Muslim brothers and sisters being treated like terrorists.
No one gives a shit if you die if your brown or black.
They've watched us suffering so much they've become immune to it,
Only caring when you palm bitches die instead.
Old white fucks thinking they have a say on dismembering our body parts with bombs,

Meaningless

Someone's lover, someone's child, someone's mother, someone's father, someone's entire world blown to bits and pieces,
Deprived of food and water,
Of humanity and sanity.
Is this not America?
What a fucked-up place.
I want to retreat, to desperately move,
To rip from it all its stolen power and oust these bastards from the land.
You white fucks!
You homophobic pricks!
You Zionists whores!
Go!
I rid you of my life,
Fuck you!
Go into the ocean and search for Atlantis,
Go into space and disrupt the stars,
Go dissipate entirely.
Become nothing but ash and less than ash,
Be nothing.
And if energy truly is never created nor destroyed, I hope to God that philosophy isn't true.
I want your energy gone from this universe.
Every inch of you forgotten and wiped clean.
You hateful sons of bitches!
You genocidal freaks!
Leave us alone.
Leave the people, the children, the beautiful, lonely people alone.

Give us our land back,
Our rights,
Our nature,
We oust you from our lives and our Earth,
Fuck off the lot of you.

June 29, 2024, 2:24 PM
Oh, I fear I am an addict.
I get so excited at the secretes I hold and offer a bigger dose.
I find myself holding secrets and lying through my teeth to even those I must be vulnerable to like a doctor,
I should be truthful,
But perhaps I just cannot recall my pains and answers.
If I do not practice first what I say how am I to answer truthfully?
I fear I have power to abuse,
Some that I do not know I hold,
Some that I do not wish to hold.
Oh, my complexity,
Oh, my versatility,
Oh, how I love it.
I have a problem keeping secretes.
I have a problem wanting bigger doses,
I have a problem knowing myself so thoroughly.
Like clear glass or a mirror held in front of me at all times,
Drugs I'll subside,

I know I will, so I sustain.
I may seem pure, but it is only because I know my faults and aggression,
I know so well that I'll die ,
I know so much I cannot tell.
Oh, my thoughts and feelings why do I hide them.
Oh goodness I am an addict for many things
I'll subside.
But I fear I am not fearful enough,
Goodness, I love myself,
And it's insanity.

June 30, 2024, 2:03 AM
I fear living in this life more and more as I see it derail,
All these laws overturned.
I feel a pit turn in my stomach.
My dreams crumble before me.
I've never meant it,
I don't think I've truly ever felt this real about it,
But if I kill myself,
I'll get out of here.
I feel myself jealous of Aaron Bushnell,
He escaped,
Brutally,
But he doesn't have to watch the entire world continue to crumble with no way to fix it.
I want to focus on my humanity,
My creativity,
My work and my life,

But this imperialism will touch me.
Assault me wherever I hide,
It'll creep on me and,
Rape me violently,
Infecting my entire being.
Never letting me go and never leaving me.
Fucking me over and over again, this state will kill
me and kill my dreams and my family.
I can't watch them anymore,
I can't stand their suffering,
Losing everything they've ever worked for,
Unable to truly save them and keep my beloveds
safe.
I've never truly thunk of it as an opportunity,
As something I'd actually do,
Even when I attempted,
Even when I planned,
But if I kill myself now,
I won't have to watch the world derail.
I could just exit.
I know,
I know,
That can't be my way out.
That should never be an option.
I have so much yet to do,
I have not yet even published.
What if I write all these words and no one ever finds
them?
Who the fuck do I think I'll be some kind of Anne
Frank?

Meaningless

I won't leave a will,
But a trail of delusions.
Written apologies,
Poems,
My works,
My fan fictions,
My mind so unanswered,
So unexplored, so unexploited, it feels like an ending of a long drama.
I really want to leave,
I'm scared,
I don't want to die.
I am not even suicidal, but I'm terrified of this war reaching me.
I'm in the middle of it,
America will fall.
By God, it'll fall and with it the calamity will destroy me to pieces.
Why, just why was my generation cursed this way, I don't want to deal with it.
Please someone stop it.
I can't enjoy my life without thinking of the impeding war.
The footsteps of soldiers lining their guns in my face,
Reaching my doorstep.
I've haven't saved any money,
I buy and buy away.
This world will end,

This environment will collapse, and I'll sit here with nothing,
Just my stupid trinkets.
I'm afraid.
A fight,
I've always wanted a fight,
But I've always had so much to lose.
Command armies,
But can't get out of bed,
Can't get out of my head.
Want to pluck my eyes out and rest.
Put a bullet through my eyes,
Hold it there for a moment let me process.
In death can I finally focus?
Can I finally sit and write?
As if my floating consciousness will have the ability to remember all my stories and find itself at peace in the afterlife to peruse my happiness.
What if I am to lose it all?
Oh, I hate thinking like this but seeing the world escalate in violence,
Reaching my front door,
It seems like the only escape.
Should I?
Could I?
I'm terrified.

A.N:
I must've been happy every July lol I didn't write anything for two years during that month.

-June 30, 2024, 2:27 AM

It's funny watching my slow derail into madness editing these.

-July 1, 2024, 6:04 PM

A. N= Author Notes